Extra Ordinary Touches for an Ordinary Day

Extraordinary Touches

Thanks for being you

for an

Ordinary Day

Jo Packham

Sterling Publishing Co., Inc. New York

A Sterling / Chapelle Book

Chapelle Ltd.:
        Owner: Jo Packham
        Editor: Laura Best

Photo stylists: Jill Dahlberg
                   Jo Packham

Photographers: Kevin Dilley, Hazen Imaging, Inc.
                  Scot Zimmerman, Scot Zimmerman Photography

Staff: Areta Bingham, Kass Burchett, Ray Cornia, Marilyn Goff,
                 Karla Haberstich, Holly Hollingsworth, Susan Jorgensen,
                 Barbara Milburn, Karmen Quinney, Cindy Stoeckl, Kim Taylor,
                 Sara Toliver, Desirée Wybrow

Library of Congress
Cataloging-in-Publication Data Available

10 9 8 7 6 5 4 3 2 1

Published by Sterling Publishing Company, Inc.
387 Park Avenue South, New York, N.Y. 10016
©2002 by Jo Packham
Distributed in Canada by Sterling Publishing
c/o Canadian Manda Group, One Atlantic Avenue, Suite 105
Toronto, Ontario, Canada M6K 3E7
Distributed in Great Britian and Europe by Cassell PLC
Wellington House, 125 Strand, London WC2R 0BB, England
Distributed in Australia by Capricorn Link (Australia) Pty. Ltd.
P.O. Box 704, Windsor, NSW 2756 Australia

Printed and Bound in China

Sterling ISBN 0-8069-5480-9

    If you have any questions or comments, please contact:

Chapelle Ltd,. Inc.
P.O. Box 9252
Ogden, UT 84409
e-mail: chapelle@chapelleltd.com
website: www.chapelleltd.com

Nothing is more precious than saying "thank you," or "I love you"—in your own way.

Contents

Introduction

*T*his is a time in which most of us sincerely believe that we are too busy for anything extra. Too busy for the little acts of thoughtfulness; too rushed to take the time to find that one small gift that is unusual or one-of-a-kind; too overwhelmed to perform those small gestures which are that little something extra and allows us to express our love, our hospitality, and our sincere appreciation for those we love, . . . whether they live with us or just come to visit and maybe stay for a day or two.

There is, however, no better time to reevaluate the reasons we find it easier simply not to do that little something extra—at least on a daily basis—for those who mean the most to us. I don't believe it is the money or even the time. I believe it is because, maybe, we simply do not know how, or when, or for what reasons. It is another instance of not knowing exactly what to do, so rather than doing it incorrectly, we choose not to do it at all.

If I were given a dollar or an extra hour of time for each little touch that I have been given, I would be regarded as one of the decadently rich with too much time on her hands. All of my adult life I have been blessed with family and friends who have done all of the "little" things to make me feel loved, appreciated, and at home regardless of where I am.

In my young adult years, my wonderful "little" (I use that term affectionately because she is a tiny little thing with beautiful white hair) mother-in-law treated all of her children and their spouses so very special. We would go to visit in the summer and, as we were sitting by the pool, she would bring us lunches that looked as if they were prepared by a gourmet deli. On holidays like Thanksgiving, she would make each family a turkey, complete with dressing and potatoes, to take home so we could have turkey sandwiches later on. I am not certain, even to this day, whether she truly loved to cook; but I know from the bottom of my heart that she loved doing nice things for all of us.

Later came my friend Martha, whom I met while my husband was in law school in California. After graduation, we returned

home to Utah; but I still visit Martha several times a year because we share more than most sisters do. When I arrive, she picks me up at the airport and whisks me off to a sidewalk café and a long lunch to catch up. She always has the refrigerator stocked with the drinks I favor, has my favorite dessert sitting on the counter with plates and forks, and makes me the most comfortable bed I have ever experienced. No matter how hard I try, I cannot duplicate her sleeping arrangements. She never forgets anything about what anyone she loves thinks is important. Before she moved from Santa Cruz, she always had reservations at my favorite restaurant on the last night of my visit and arranged for a very large to-go box so I could carry extra servings home on the plane.

Next came my friend Candace, who started out as my boss and mentor. After our working together came to an end, we became lasting friends. Whenever I visit her in New York, her key is waiting with the doorman so I do not have to be announced. My bed is turned down and the closet is emptied for my things to be put away—as if I would stay forever. She helps me with my career problems, listens long into the night about my personal life, and always invites me back with a long hug and a very sincere I Love You.

Claudia is a former college roommate who moved away and made certain we never lost touch. Whenever a business trip calls me to the Philadelphia area, she has my room waiting, fresh towels in the bath, and bagels in the fridge. She makes home-cooked meals and chauffeurs me from one show to the next, regardless of the hours of the day. She always has a smile, an encouraging word, and a new place to take me "antiquing."

Linda is my lifelong friend. She is probably the ultimate hostess and has taught us all the finer points about making everyone feel welcome. At her ranch, she has a bunkhouse for guests, which she built right next to the river. Each little cottage has its own separate kitchen, bathroom, radio, and television—complete with vcr and a large selection of movies. The door to the main house is always open, there is a picture of her with me in the living room with the rest of her family photographs. Her furnishings are elegant, yet she has a way of making me feel like it really is fine to put my feet on the table!

What is it about these "extraordinary touches for the ordinary days" that makes us feel special, comfortable, and at home? Why do such special touches—large or small, obvious or discreet, exquisitely crafted or mass-produced, intentional or second nature—immediately convey a myriad of sentiments? Perhaps, it is because such thoughtful touches or tiny treasures invariably bear the stamp of the individual heart and hand that created and gave them away.

This is, therefore, why I am offering in the pages of this book a compilation of ideas and inspiration for decorating and creating special touches to teach others what to do, when to do it, and how easy it is to make someone you care about feel like everyday is a very special day, indeed.

Forever,
Jo

Making a Home

Fresh flowers anywhere and everywhere will not only bring color and beauty into the room, they will help replenish the room's fresh air. When you go to the garden to cut the flowers you have tended or to the florist to buy the favored flowers of the week, make certain to choose a different flower than last week's. Select someone's favorite, choose a color to match a room, or buy for the fragrance alone. Each of these selections makes an extraordinary touch for an ordinary day.

We can do many special things for our family; some are quite common and very visible, while others are invisible and often unnoticed. Doing the "little things" in our homes will make our family members' lives healthier and happier when they may never even know why.

To create a healthy home that offers joy, vitality, and social interaction, while promoting relaxation and deep healing sleep, try the following suggestions:

1. The term of the new millennium is "simplify." Clutter and disorder have been proven to be major sources of uneasiness and stress, and to bring feelings of inhibition for certain personality types. In rooms where family members spend time, declutter shelves and floor areas. If you add something new, remember to take something away. For those family members who feel "empty" with too much space and need to be surrounded by "lots of stuff," give them a room with which to do exactly as they like.

2. Decorate naturally by keeping it simple and bringing the outside in whenever possible. Enhance any room with green plants and fresh flowers. Be certain to keep them trimmed and in clean water. Well-kept plants will add beauty and joy while cleansing the air for your family and friends to breathe. Use other decorative items that impact individual moods, such as candles, soft music, and good food. These special touches can help your family and guests feel and do their best both at home and while they are away.

3. Be certain there is fresh air circulating throughout your home for a minimum of two hours per day. Whatever the weather or

the temperature is outside, ensure a constant supply of fresh air by opening windows or doors at opposite ends of your home to encourage natural ventilation.

4. Whenever possible, use natural light. Access to sunlight accomplishes several goals: it improves personal psychological well being; it helps the body's internal clock run smoothly; and it makes any room warm, bright, and welcoming.

LEFT: Using "special pieces" in areas of the home gives each family member a feeling of ownership and pride.

RIGHT: Pillows, blankets, and soft leather make an inviting combination in a comfortable family room.

BOTTOM: Bright, rainbow colors not only bring color and warmth into a room, but are the best for concealing dirt and wear.

5. When decorating, choose decorative accent pieces that have meaning for every member of the family and close friends. An obvious way is to decorate with photographs of the people, places, and times that mean the most. Other ideas might be family collections, memorabilia from family sports and hobbies, or just the "little things" that someone special loves.

6. Choose the colors in each and every room carefully and individually. Color has an enormous subliminal impact on a person's mood as well as the way he or she reacts to other individuals. Neutrals and cool colors give a restful, calm quality and are the appropriate colors for areas of relaxation, sleep, and quiet interaction. Warm colors, which encourage activity or movement and lighten personalities, should be used in rooms where family gatherings and activities take place.

7. Use natural products and fibers throughout the home. Floors should be wood or types of marble or stone. Fabrics should be cottons and linens. Cleaners should be organic. Furniture pieces should be made of natural woods and fibers. Be certain furniture is comfortable, of good quality, and appropriate for the needs of the family.

Display pictures and memorabilia of times together with friends and family. Be certain your guest is represented in the groupings.

Minding Your Manners

Your home is a sanctuary for both your family and the guests you invite to visit or to stay. Whether you are the guest, the host, or a family member, there are manners that are not only appropriate but essential when guests come to visit—or anytime. The rules are simple and apply to everyone.

1. Before you invite someone to stay, be aware of their feelings towards animals. Not everyone loves your pet and some may have allergies to certain species. Be certain that guests know which animals you have, how many there are, and how involved in the family they are before the guests are invited. If you are a guest, do not bring your pet unless you are specifically invited to do so by your host.

2. Communicate and adhere to the itinerary or time schedule you have planned. If you are arriving, leaving, or joining someone, be certain to be punctual. Avoid deviating from your schedule unless you give ample notice—others are making plans around you so be sensitive to their time.

3. Let your host or guests know if there are "other" plans during the visit. If you have a scheduled time with others or want time for yourself, tell the host or guests in advance. Where appropriate, invite them along or make suggestions for activities they might engage in while you are gone.

4. Do not make unreasonable requests of your host or your guest, such as food that is difficult to cook, places to see that are difficult to reach, or activities that are expensive or in which the entertainment is based solely on personal preference.

ABOVE: Be certain to respond to any invitations as soon as possible. Inform your host whether you will be attending and any information about the arrival and departure times as well as activities planned during the visit.

RIGHT: Be conscious of time. Be punctual and follow the agreed schedule arranged between you and your guest or host. If changes must be made, give as much notice as possible for new arrangements.

5. Use common sense in regard to a dress code. Neither host nor guest should run around the house in pajamas. Casual clothes or sweats should be worn to breakfast and during the evenings that are spent at home.

6. In regards to alcohol and tobacco, the guest should abstain if the host does. Do not smoke in or around the house and do not ask for wine with dinner or a beer during the movie if your host does not partake of such substances.

7. If you are the guest, ask before using the telephone, television, or stereo. Charge telephone calls to your home number or credit card—even if your host insists that you do not. Let the host regulate the remote control, select the movies to watch, and pick the style of music played.

8. Refrain from borrowing things from your guest or your host. If you must borrow items, be certain to return them immediately after use. If you break something, be certain the owner is told and that it is repaired or replaced. You should do more than just offer; you should quietly follow through to make certain it is done. If it cannot be repaired or replaced, purchase something else of equal or greater value that the owner may need or want.

9. Have a visitor's gift waiting upon his or her arrival. It can be a small memento like a journal with a nice writing pen, a disposable camera with a scrapbook, or a framed picture of the two of you when you were young or the last time you were together.

15

10. As a guest, be certain to participate in minor chores. Help prepare the meals—whether that be picking fresh vegetables from the garden or whipping mashed potatoes. Help clear the table after each meal and participate in washing the dishes.

Make your bed every morning. When your visit is over, take the sheets off your bed and stack them on the washing machine. Fold bedspread and blankets neatly at the end of the bed and stack the pillows on top.

Keep showers to a minimum and keep the bathroom spotless after each use. Avoid keeping toiletries in the bathroom unless you are given your own drawer. Keep your clothes picked up and put away. If you are not given a separate drawer or closet, keep them folded neatly in your closed suitcase. Participating in daily family tasks makes the stay more enjoyable for everyone.

11. As your mother constantly reminded you, always say please and thank you and never complain. Find something to sincerely compliment, regardless of how insignificant.

12. *It is proper to give the hostess a gift—whether you bring one with you, buy one while you are there, or send one within a few days upon your return home.*

13. *It is traditional for the guest to write a note and give a small gift to the hostess, but it is equally as nice for the hostess to write a thank-you note to the guest. How nice it would be to mail a note to thank someone for sharing their valuable vacation time with you and telling him or her how much the newly created memories mean to you. It is always appreciated when you hear that you were the "perfect guest" and your return is a much anticipated event.*

17

Entry

W hat says more about who lives inside than the front of someone's home? If the front gate is left open, family, friends, and neighbors feel welcome. If on the front porch there are chairs to sit in, an invitation to stay awhile is extended.

It is a shame that many homes today do not have the large old-fashioned porches found on older homes. Gone are the evenings spent rocking on the porch and talking to neighbors as they walked by. If neighbors felt welcome, if there was a place to sit for a while and rest, would these not be extraordinary touches for very ordinary days?

Welcome

Welcoming Porches

Whenever you think of "going home," the feelings of peace, comfort, and security should be what come to mind. Whether you live there now, or grew up and moved away, home should be where your heart is and where the extraordinary touches on ordinary days begin and are a way of daily living.

In such a home, it all begins with the entry through the open gate, past the chairs on the porch, and as you enter a front door that always says "welcome home" in its own style. The door can actually have a small sign printed for visitors or guests when they arrive, or it can display a seasonal wreath, a fancy knocker, or be painted with warm and welcoming colors.

In the summertime, the outside entry to your home can be filled with the garden flowers of the season. Fall can bring oversized pots filled with branches of autumn leaves, and baskets of apples and squash. Winter can fill a porch with tiny white twinkling lights and decorated potted trees that are covered with natural ornaments such as pinecones and small treats for the birds.

The Entry Doorway

The entry is the first insight into your home and family and the last image as someone leaves. It is the transition from the outside world to a place where a visit is anticipated and everyone is welcome. The entry is where the extraordinary touches for every ordinary day begin.

Such special touches can be a chair placed close by the front door. When older family members or visitors come and go, they often need a place to sit while everyone says their long-awaited welcomings or their extended goodbyes. The time of hugs and kisses may seem too short to some; but for those who are unable to stand for very long, a conveniently situated chair can ensure that they continue to be part of the festivities, yet comfortable and unhurried.

When the front door is entered, the sights, smells, and sounds should all extend a quiet welcome. It is here that the first scents of home should be experienced. These can come from vases of fresh flowers, bowls of constantly changing pot-pourri, or scented rings on lighted lamps. Quiet music can be played here, a small fountain can always be left on, or delicate chimes can be attached to the front door.

We do not often think about taking pictures of day-to-day life, or having a camera always available for unexpected special moments. It is such a nice idea to have a disposable camera sitting someplace obvious and convenient—you will be pleasantly surprised at how many candid moments can be added to the family photo albums.

It is both a good idea and an easy one to offer family and friends that which is given at quaint country inns, charming bed and breakfasts, and the finest big-city hotels. Leave an extra set of car and house keys in the event someone misplaces theirs, leave a standard pair of reading glasses and any information about events in the city, directions, or important local addresses. Not only do visitors and overnight guests find such items helpful, but I am surprised at how often my teenage son needs to know the directions to someplace close by.

There are many items that can be kept by the front door for family and guests. A small table or shelf that holds a bouquet of flowers and a small lamp can be a convenient and an easily remembered place for everyone to drop off their keys. It is also a perfect place to leave notes for family and guests and small cards to say thank you just for being you.

It is important to leave a small lamp lit by the front door—there is nothing quite as lonely as coming home to a dark house. The lamp, always lit, will welcome them home and help light their way.

21

The entry way is a great place to leave helpful information for guests. On a table in a notebook, you can list places to go in the community, the times they are open, and directions on how to get there: recreation areas, cultural centers, restaurants, movie theaters, shopping areas, and grocery stores.

You can also list important information concerning your home: where certain items are located and how to operate each one.

Make certain to include the following vital information:

1. Names, addresses, and telephone numbers for a family doctor, nearest hospital, police, close family member, nearest neighbor, animal hospital, and veterinarian.

2. Where to find and/or how to operate: a first aid kit and fire extinguisher; fuse box location; controls for the heater and air conditioner; the washer, dryer, iron, and ironing board; the oven and microwave; the garbage dumpster (if you are visiting someone in a big city apartment, finding their trash receptacles is a challenge); the switch for the garbage disposal; extra pillows, blankets, and towels; the telephone book; and extra keys to the house and the car.

If you are a believer of the principles of Fung Shui, you will place your floor coverings in your entry way so that they influence visitors and family members to come in, sit down, and relax. Rugs and carpets will encourage such behavior, while wood and tile floors should be used uncovered only where you want people to keep moving. It is also believed that even though you do not consciously look down, subconsciously you move in the direction of the rugs on the floor. You, therefore, want to angle your rug in the direction you wish your guests to go.

The Back Door

Traditionally the back door is most often used by close friends and family members because they are the ones who are most familiar and most comfortable with your home. Which is why it is an extraordinary touch to offer items near the back door that might make their day a little easier.

Hang a selection of coats, hats, and bags for anyone to use as needed when stepping outside. A collection of umbrellas and walking sticks are often forgotten until the weather is seen through the back-door screen, so having them close at hand makes life simpler.

The sights and smells encountered when coming in or going out of the back door should be as welcoming as the front. This aroma is most associated with warm baked cookies or freshly brewed coffee. A drop of vanilla extract on a lit light bulb or potpourri simmering in a kettle on the stove can keep these same aromas in the room throughout the day. Comforting colors such as wedgewood blue and butter yellow invite one in to linger or invite them back.

A bench or rug by the back door, on which to leave footware, quietly welcomes guests and family members to take off their shoes and relax. In today's busy world, no more needs to be said in regard to keeping your home as clean as possible for as long as possible.

Kitchen

Have a snack of seasonal fresh fruit along with serving utensils on the counter for when anyone gets hungry during the day.

24

The kitchen is the ultimate gathering place associated with comforts such as home-cooking, loved ones, and times of sharing. To make your kitchen as lovely as it is practical, fill unexpected places with fresh flowers and treasured family heirlooms. Use the crockery bowl in which your grandmother prepared her signature apple pie to hold your freshly picked garden vegetables while they ripen. Place a tiny night-light on the cutting board your son made in wood shop. By using family-made pieces, you are inviting old and happy memories into the room for all to share.

The kitchen and the meals that are prepared there present the perfect time and place to add an often-overlooked special touch. When I was first married, my mother-in-law taught me more about being a thoughtful and gracious hostess than I could have learned in a thousand pages of reading about entertaining or etiquette. She always had glasses stored in the freezer compartment of her refrigerator so that when cold drinks were served, they were indeed as cold as they could be. And when a warm dinner was served, it was served on plates that had been heated in the oven while the meal was being prepared. It is a practice used in the finest restaurants around the world but seldom thought of to be used with family or friends.

Everyone naturally gravitates toward the kitchen, so it is a nice gesture to have dishes, silverware, and a bowl of fruit or other snacks set out on the kitchen counter. When family members come home from work or school, or when overnight guests come looking for an afternoon snack, but are too timid to ask, such a gesture is always welcome. Also be certain to have ample seating for those drifting in and lingering while you are preparing tea for two or dinner for eight.

As guests drift into the kitchen, offer to share your recipe for the evening fare with them. A handwritten recipe card including the makings and necessary preparation plus a small note about how happy you are to have them as part of your "family" will become a pleasant memory of their visit.

Bring the sounds of music into your kitchen, matching the musical selection with what you are preparing. Pasta can be prepared to the sounds of Luciano Pavarotti, or you can shake a martini to Frank Sinatra. A small CD collection and player in the kitchen will add joy and flavor to any culinary experience for both the cook and family or friends.

LEFT: Chill glasses in the freezer to serve cold drinks.

BELOW: Warm plates and bowls in the oven before serving a hot dinner to keep the meal warm.

BOTTOM: Keep a night-light on in the kitchen to aid guests, whether getting a glass of water or enjoying the last piece of cake.

Morning Meal

Mornings are often a hurried time of day for everyone in any household. Teenagers are in a frenzy to leave for school, parents are rushing to work, and guests are in a hurry to begin their day—so very few enjoy the quiet moments that the beginning of a new day should bring. Make this time simpler by putting everything out the night before. Rise a few minutes early to retrieve the paper; prepare the coffee, juice, or hot chocolate; and toast the bagels or cut up the fruit. This will help everyone you care about start the day the way it should be—quiet, unhurried, healthy, and happy.

Amber Tea Delight

2 cups boiling water
2 tea bags
1 12-oz. can apricot nectar
1 cup orange juice concentrate
¼ cup sugar
¼ cup lemon juice
2 cups ginger ale, chilled

In a teapot pour boiling water over tea bags; cover and let stand 5 minutes. Remove tea bags; cool. In a medium pitcher, combine cooled tea, apricot nectar, orange juice, sugar, and lemon juice. Cover and chill. Just before serving, stir in ginger ale. Serve in ice-filled glasses.

Special Treats

More often than not when food is prepared on a daily basis, only the necessary is attended to. How nice it would be for everyone if a few special touches were added—for no reason at all. Cut-up lemons, limes, or oranges added to a pitcher of ice water that is set on the table for the dinner meal, flavored nectars or a sprig of fresh mint added to a specially made iced tea, or fresh fruit served in gently whipped cream with shredded coconut are flavorful touches that will be delightfully enjoyed.

Once in a while make mealtimes special with colorful table settings, using place mats and utensils from different countries or cultures.

Luncheons

When serving your family lunch, present it as if you were having guests over. Set the meal on a kitchen island so the family can serve themselves buffet style. Wrap freshly baked bread (or warmed store-bought bread will work just as well) in linen towels. Monogram a cake with powdered sugar. In place of soda serve a blended fresh-fruit drink with mint. Use unusual serving dishes for a special salad, and add a beautiful tablecloth with a small bouquet of fresh flowers. It doesn't take any longer to create a special family luncheon than it does to set the table.

Pear Salad

Dressing
3 Tbls. sugar or honey
1 tsp. salt
Pepper to taste
¼ cup salad oil
¼ cup red wine vinegar
1 Tbls. sesame oil

Using a shaker, mix all dressing ingredients together. Store overnight in fridge.

Salad
4 cups spring lettuce mix
½ head iceberg lettuce
1 seedless cucumber, cut in quarters and sliced
2 red pears, cored, sliced thin
½ cup craisins, sliced
4 Tbls. feta cheese, crumbled
4 Tbls. pecans, broken

On individual plates, place spring mix, lettuce, and cucumber. Place pear slices on top of greens. Sprinkle cheese, craisins, and pecans over top. Drizzle dressing over complete salad to taste.

Dining Room

Sitting down for dinner in a formal dining room with a table set as if it were a holiday is not something that is done by very many families in this day of different schedules and hurried life-styles. Some analysts and psychologists believe that this very lack of sitting down to a more formal family dinner is one of the major causes of the demise of the family.

It is important to set the dining-room table, turn off the television, light the candles, and serve dinner as if it were a special occasion, even though it is just an ordinary Tuesday evening. If you do just this one extra touch once or twice a week, you will be surprised how conscientious your family becomes when it is time to be home for dinner. Also, if you are quiet and listen carefully, you will be surprised how much you learn about each other.

There are additional small touches that you can add to your table settings. Make subtle seating assignments with different kinds of place cards, allowing everyone to sit by someone new in the family and maybe mend some delicate issues or bring two members closer.

One place card your family will enjoy the most is to use photographs of the person who is to sit in each particular seat. One evening they can be current pictures that are your particular favorites; another evening they can be candid shots that will make everyone laugh; and still another could be the baby pictures of everyone at the table.

Candles are another nice addition to the table; however, be careful as to the size, type, and scent of the candles that you select. Small candles burn too quickly and tall tapers drip onto the tablecloth. The candles should be unscented, or scented with a flavor that accentuates the evening meal.

Cloth napkins with napkin rings; an eclectic array of dishes, glasses, and serving pieces; and the good silverware all help to make each dinner an event that is a very nice time in an often not-so-nice day.

Create a special family event in the middle of an ordinary week by setting the dining-room table as if it were a holiday, and celebrate the family.

Special Settings

In addition to setting a special table for your family, consider inviting neighbors or close friends over for no reason at all and treat them as if it were a special evening indeed. During the summer months, decorate the table for girlfriends in roses and white linen. Tuck a fresh flower or write a short note to each friend, then place it in their folded napkin and use it as a place card. Have a small gift at each plate to say thank you for "just being you."

This nonoccasion should be celebrated in an inviting atmosphere which will soothe the soul and uplift the spirit. This is the opportunity to enhance the act of fine dining, invite guests to linger for a while, and create new traditions.

ABOVE LEFT: When inviting over friends with younger children, let them create their own place mat or name tag while they wait for the meal to be prepared, allowing parents time to socialize peacefully.

ABOVE RIGHT: Involve children when making a toast. Fill their glasses with a nonalcoholic beverage they may enjoy.

Displaying family treasures and heirlooms is one way of making the original heirloom owner feel very loved indeed. Dishes passed from mother to daughter for several generations, linens with hand-embroidered designs, a grouping of unique picture frames, or a collection of Santa Clauses brings personality and sharing of beloved and cherished articles into the dining room.

*I*t is important that a living room fit the needs and life-style of the family that uses it—or should use it. To decorate the living room so it can truly be shared and enjoyed is a special touch for every ordinary day.

This family enjoys a formal living room arranged in several conversation groups. Two people can sit in front of the fireplace and have a private discussion while additional family members or friends can be in the same room yet separated and involved in their own conversation. Because of the arrangement of furniture, everyone is able to enjoy the fire and the feeling of being involved and belonging while enjoying a certain amount of privacy.

Though many prefer their living room more formal and use it for entertaining guests, there is no reason everyone can't enjoy this room on a daily basis. This is the room that should invite all to relax and enjoy life with each other. This is the one room in your home that regardless of style should be comfortable and put everyone who enters at ease. Have at least one sitting area to encourage conversing, reading, or taking a glance at the evening paper. Also arrange the room to accommodate watching television, taking naps, playing games, or working on needlework or other hobbies.

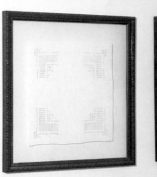

RIGHT TOP: Keep family treasures close at hand, such as these precious framed handkerchiefs showing grandmother's crocheting and embroidering skills.

RIGHT BOTTOM: Plants, whether flowers or greenery, bring life and freshness into a room. Be certain to change plants often to keep them fresh.

Lighting can change the feel of a room. A welcoming glow in the living room is important. Encourage a warm, close feeling by using the fireplace along with the light of a number of burning candles.

During the daylight hours, regardless of the season, let the sun shine into the room whenever possible. This natural light adds a sense of wellbeing to the room and those inside.

Have plenty of pillows and comfortable seating. Keep important momentos and family-made treasures visible for all to enjoy while showing each member how important they are in the family.

A fireplace is an addition to the living room that is appreciated by all who enter. Whenever the air turns chilly—whether morning or evening, midweek or holiday—light a fire for all to enjoy.

These families enjoy living rooms that are less formal and more massive in nature and appearance. They are however, decorated and arranged to give family members and friends a sense of intimacy and belonging.

Conversation groupings, gaming tables, and fireplaces all invite someone to sit and stay for awhile.

The manner in which a room is decorated is not often thought of as an extraordinary touch; but to those who have endured evenings being entertained in rooms that are stiff and uncomfortable, it is a thoughtful consideration indeed for family and friends to be able to enjoy all of the rooms in a home.

Family Room

Create a special box for family members to receive or give cherished notes and cards from one another. Display the box in a prominent area of the family room to encourage and remind members of the family to remember each other often. When company comes, the box can be closed and still add to the décor of the room without giving away the contents meant exclusively for family members.

*T*he mood of a family room is determined by a variety of elements and how these elements interact with each other and the family members themselves. The feel of the room can be changed by the type of lighting used. The lights need to be varied and independent. Sometimes the lighting needs to be low so as to enjoy the television or a movie. Sometimes the lighting needs to be brighter so that games can be played or hobbies completed. Sometimes the lighting needs to be warm and subtle so that one can leave the "glare" of the day behind.

Music is another way to change or enhance the mood of the room. Have a selection of music available that appeals to every family member and their varying activities or moods.

Freely display photographs of special people and memorable occasions throughout the room—whether as a grouping or scattered strategically. Coordinate collections of matching frames or mix eclectic sizes, shapes, and themes—as varied as the people and places in the pictures themselves. Whether a family member or a friend, nothing makes a person feel more loved or important than to see their picture displayed in prominent places.

Special treasures that are collected by each member of the family, hankies, books, teacups, shells, or baskets—can be arranged around the room, representing things that are beautiful to each individual who uses and enjoys this room in the home.

Not everything in the family's comfort space must be perfectly matched or part of a set. The furniture pieces and objects that each family member finds comfortable and needed can be placed together in a creative way.

LEFT: Turn a favorite photograph into a place mat to be used in the family room—protecting the furniture from day-to-day living and to subtly remind your children how much you enjoy not only them but the friends they bring home.

41

The family room is an important room to let the natural sun shine in and let the fresh air in for at least a little while each and every day. Both of these natural elements add to the health and well-being of everyone.

Fresh water, always available in a funky seltzer bottle, can act as a decorating accent as well as a much appreciated thirst quencher.

The family room is normally used to enjoy any number of board and card games with friends and family members.

Hang a hammock inside and bring the outdoors in for family members to enjoy the "calm and relaxation of a quiet summer afternoon" regardless of the temperature outside.

Study

A den or study is one room in the house that is truly personal and should be designed with the primary user in mind. It is not a room that should be filled with books that are never read, a desk that is unusable with a chair that is uncomfortable, or lighting that is either too bright or too soft. Here is a room where the owner can continue his or her work in a quiet, creative environment, relax and recharge after a hectic day, or spend time enriching a depleted soul.

Create an office with comfortable furniture. There should be more than one type of chair so that each type of activity can be accommodated. There may be a couch for entertaining or relaxing. Using chairs and a couch made from natural fibers, with good supports and comfortable pillows, surrounded by adequate lighting makes this room more inviting and livable.

A source for natural light and fresh air should be available somewhere in the room. Consider changes is temperature and place comfortable throws of different weights around the room to be used as needed.

Make certain there are books placed around the room that are new and of interest to family members or guests. Make certain that all of the equipment necessary in an efficient study is present: reading glasses, a magnifying glass, a letter opener, stamps, papers—both lined and unlined; pens, pencils and markers; eraser, elastic bands, paper clips, scissors, rulers, file folders, envelopes, and a drawer that locks. All of these additions may seem obvious, but making certain they are in place and always replaced is one of those extraordinary touches for an ordinary day.

Using a favorite collection such as shells to dress up necessary items brings focus, unity, and personality into a room which is otherwise filled with sterile work materials.

Many women use their den as a home office. If this is the case, work papers, files, and computer disks do not have to clutter up this room to still make it functional. Use a selection of baskets and trays to hold office supplies and correspondence. A small dresser can double as a compartment for important invoices, forms, or documents. If these items are stored cleverly in corresponding baskets and decorative boxes, this room can be a comfortable retreat rather than a work room if one needs a place to merely escape.

Below is a list of liquors and mixes that the average host will need to make the drinks most often requested.

Liquors:
Beer
Bourbon
Cognac or other
    brandy
Gin (London dry)
Rum (light)
Rye or Canadian
    whiskey
Scotch whiskey
Tequila
Vermouth: dry
    & sweet Vodka
Wine: white & red

Garnishes:
Cocktail onions
Green olives
Lemons, limes,
    oranges

Mixers & flavorings:
Club soda
Cola
Ginger ale
Tonic water
Lemon-lime soda
Cranberry juice
Grapefruit juice
Orange juice
Pineapple juice
Tomato juice
Bitters
Grenadine
Maraschino liqueur
Worchestershire sauce
Salt and pepper
Sugar
Tabasco sauce

Accouterments:
Ice bucket with ice
Short straws
Swizzle sticks
Toothpicks

A Den For Him

Each den or study should have a selection of beverages. Whether the refreshment is bottled water or alcoholic in nature, the assortment should be fresh and appropriate. There should be an ice bucket that can be easily filled and a selection of glasses for each beverage, with an array of snacks. It is a nice touch for the person using this room.

Fresh flowers and candles, as well as a selection of music and an appropriate sound system, should be within reach. It is also essential that a television, vcr, and assortment of videos be available. After all, this is a room for many uses and all that is needed for working, relaxing, and entertainment should be accessible and complete.

If there is a bar in the study or den, try arranging the chairs so that they are not facing the bar and pushed in so that they look uninviting. Pull the chairs out and turn them slightly as if they are ready for an evening of private conversation.

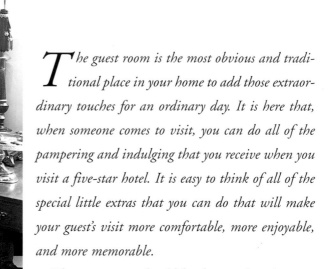

Guest Room

*T*he guest room is the most obvious and traditional place in your home to add those extraordinary touches for an ordinary day. It is here that, when someone comes to visit, you can do all of the pampering and indulging that you receive when you visit a five-star hotel. It is easy to think of all of the special little extras that you can do that will make your guest's visit more comfortable, more enjoyable, and more memorable.

The guest room should be decorated so that it is comfortable and usable for guests. You will want to have a king-size bed with an extra chair so guests will not be crowded. When they arrive, have a small serving tray on the bed filled with fresh flowers, a warm or cold drink, and snacks—depending on the season. They normally are tired and hungry after traveling and this will be the perfect little extra to refresh them.

The guest room should be beautifully decorated but not overdone. An abundance of pillows on the bed is pretty to look at but a challenge to unmake at bedtime and remake in the morning. Put only enough extras to add your signature touch.

The individual habits of both the guest and the host will dictate how much time a guest will spend in their room. Be certain that, whether this be a considerable amount of time or only those moments before and after they retire, they will have available anything that they might need.

A comfortable chair and a good light for reading are essential to the convenience of your guest. Also have a selection of good books that will appeal to your visitor and a selection of reading glasses and a magnifying glass. A small vase of fresh flowers should be placed in as many places in the room as the room décor will allow. There is nothing more welcoming, or says more without saying anything, than a bouquet of fresh flowers. Be careful, however, in regard to the types of flowers you select. Avoid arranging flowers with a strong scent, even if they are your favorite. If your guest cannot tolerate the strong scent of lavender or lilies, you do not want to make them uncomfortable.

Also make certain there is a telephone in the guest room. Have a local telephone book and directions for calling long distance if there are special instructions for your area. It is important that the telephone be in the guest room so that they can speak in private and at times that are convenient for them.

Be considerate of the needs of your guests and make certain there is a small desk or writing area in their room. Supply writing papers and pens, envelopes and stamps, and a good light with a comfortable chair. If the room is a small one, this is also the perfect location for books and a small bulletin-type board with pins for them to display schedules or meeting times in a place that they will not forget.

It is essential that the temperature in the room be comfortable for your guests; and what that perfect temperature might be is always difficult to prejudge. To cover every contingency, have a fan above the bed in the room. If your guests are too warm or the room feels stuffy, it is easy to increase the circulation by turning on the fan. Make certain the room has a screened window that provides natural light and fresh air. It is important that the guest be able to open it and that it can be locked.

closets
&
Drawers

In the guest room, the closets and drawers are an important aspect of a comfortable stay. The closet should always be at least half empty with an adequate supply of hangers so guests have a place to hang their clothing. The other half of the closet should be filled with an assortment of sweaters

and coats of different weights and styles so that if the temperature changes or the guests are unprepared, they have the proper clothing available to wear during their stay. This is also the perfect place to supply your guests with umbrellas, hats, scarves, and any other accessories that are appropriate for the weather in your area.

In the top of the closet, keep an extra supply of pillows, linens, and bedding. Place or hang a sachet in the closet so that when the guest opens the closet door, it does not smell musty.

Make certain there is at least one empty drawer that they can use. It is best to have one large drawer and one smaller drawer emptied for their use. Because the guest room is not used as often as other rooms in the home, have the drawers lined with softly scented papers or place a sachet in the drawer to keep it fresh between uses.

small Touches

An easy way to decorate your guest room without a tremendous amount of expense is to use the items your guest might need as the accent pieces for the room. Extra linens, pillows, and blankets placed in a variety of baskets around the room are beautiful to look at and easy for the guests to use. This solves the decorating and storage problems if your guest room is small.

Make certain the guest room has an alarm clock that is easy to use. It is embarrassing for your guest to have to ask you to wake them at a certain time—especially if they have an early flight or meeting and would rather not disturb the rest of the family.

Display around the room items that will bring a smile to the guest's face. A framed picture of the guest and host from years ago is especially appreciated, reminding both how long they have been friends.

Turn the guest room into a quiet retreat. A special touch that is easy to create for your guest room—one that will be both used and appreciated—is a window seat. Simply take a bench and place it under a window. Add a shawl, a good book, and a cool drink and you have created a place that your guests will enjoy anytime of the day or night.

For added privacy, a small "Do Not Disturb" sign is a nice idea to put on the inside of the guest-room door. That way, if they are not feeling well, or wish to take a nap or sleep in, they can hang it on the outside of the door, letting you know they wish to be left alone.

53

A well-supplied guest room is one of the easiest ways to make your guests stay as comfortable and as enjoyable as possible. A large armoire in the guest room will hold a great deal of what will keep your guest entertained, yet can be closed to keep it from cluttering the room. Inside the armoire,

have a television, a vcr, and a selection of movies. Make certain there are instructions on how to run both the television and the vcr in the event the guest in unfamiliar with the workings.

The armoire is also a perfect place to keep an assortment of boxes filled with extras that your guest might find helpful. Have the boxes labeled so that the guest does not feel as if they are snooping to see what is inside.

It is here that you can keep a fire extinguisher, flashlight, candles, matches, a house map with instructions, and any other items that are important during an emergency.

If you do not have room in your guest quarters for a small desk, this is a good place to keep supplies for writing notes, making lists, etc.

In every room in the home, but especially in the guest room, it is important to have a small night-light. In this guest room, the small wooden church atop the armoire stays lit throughout the night to keep the guest safe. It is also a nice idea to place an angel somewhere in your guest room to give your family and friends the feeling of being cared for.

Light refreshments such as wine and fresh fruit or hot tea and cookies, depending on the season, are always appreciated. Prepare a tray and place it in the guest's room while they are away as a unexpected surprise on their return. Be aware not to have snacks interfere with meal plans. If uncertain of plans, fill a basket with snacks that can keep until the guest is ready.

snacks

Try to anticipate the needs of your guests so that you can offer everything they might wish for or need without their having to ask. A small refrigerator either in the guest room, or near enough to the guest room that they know its contents are there specifically for them, will make your guests stay very comfortable indeed.

When you are a guest it seems that you get hungry at the most inopportune times. If your host is thoughtful enough to make these items available any time during the day or night, your visit is one that is filled with small indulgences and thoughtful gestures that you will not soon forget.

Stock the refrigerator as if it were a hotel mini bar. Include:
- glasses
- A filled ice bucket
- Juices
- Assorted soft drinks
- Bottled water
- A selection of wines & liquors
- Snacks such as yogurt, candy bars, fresh fruit, cheese slices, etc.

Stock a small cupboard with utensils and goodies. Include:
- glasses & cups
- Plates & bowls
- Silverware
- Serving dishes
- Napkins
- Toothpicks
- Straws
- Snacks such as chips, kippers, nuts, pretzels, licorice

56

Whenever your guest leaves for the day, have a fresh tray of flowers, drinks, and a small snack waiting for them upon their return. If the weather is cold and dreary, a hot cup of coffee or cocoa will be ever so welcome. If the weather is hot and muggy, a tall glass of lemonade, iced tea, or chilled bottled water will be much appreciated.

It is also a nice idea to serve lunch "in" to a special visitor. Prepare a tray of cheese and crackers or tea sandwiches and serve them in her room to eat at her leisure while she dresses or reads a good book.

House Information

In a decorative box next to the guest's bed, place important information that may be helpful for someone not familiar with your house.

If there is no desk in the room, this box would also be an ideal place to keep stationery, stamps, a pen, and other materials guests may appreciate during their stay.

contents in box should include:
- closest exit
- Emergency phone numbers
- Your address & phone number
- Location of power box
- Location of fire extinguishers
- Where to find: vacuum, iron, air conditioner & heat controls

A Guest Room For Her

It is truly the small touches that you add to a guest room that will be remembered the most—especially by your female guests. A small hanging vase with fresh flowers is a welcome that most guests will not soon forget. A pretty hat that can actually be worn on sunny days, an extra pillow in a comfortable chair, and scented shells are all touches that are unnecessary yet make for a very special visit.

You can never add too many feminine touches to a room where a "girlfriend" is staying. Vintage books of the classics are fun to read on vacation, and an antique teacup with a sweet smelling rose is very special.

A small table in a guest room can say so much without saying anything at all. The small fountain on this table soothes your guest to sleep with the calming sound of running water. If this is not a welcome sound, it is easily turned off and enjoyed only for visual accents.

The doll by the fountain is a special handmade piece that was selected especially for the recipient—the tag on her hand reads: A magical friend who reminds you of what is in your heart when your heart cannot remember.

There is also a picture in the room of the guest and the hostess, which is a touch that is very important. Nothing makes someone feel more welcome or more loved than seeing her picture in the home of her friend or loved ones.

This table also holds a gift that was given to the host from the guest on a former visit. We all want to think our gifts are appreciated and loved; and when they are displayed in a prominent place in the home, we know they are treasured without having to be told.

In the guest room it is also nice to leave a small gift for the guest to take home. In this window a potted bulb is always growing so that the guest may take it home and plant in her own garden. In the spring as the tulips bloom, times spent together are remembered over and over again.

61

Most of your female friends will love the small feminine touches that you add to their guest room. A display of antique pieces that are actually to be used is a very thoughtful gesture. A carafe filled with iced water, lovely linen and lace hand towels, and a strand of pearls just in case theirs were forgotten. It is also nice to put a small dish of mints by their bedside and fragrant soaps for their use.

When packing for a trip, it is almost impossible to pack items such as robes and slippers. When these are left in the guest room for your guest to use, she will feel as if she is staying at one of the world's finest destination spas. Leave these comfortable items in a place that your guest will know they are available for her use. Also have a selection of lotions and perfumes offered in a variety of pretty bottles for your guest to indulge herself.

Guest Bath

Though a room of utility, the guest bathroom is also an intimate retreat for luxury and personal pampering. This is a space that is highly personal in your home; so you want to decorate it and fill it with items that will make your guests feel at home. This room, like the guest bedroom, is especially easy to add extraordinary touches for an ordinary day.

Display items that your guests may use as decorative accents throughout the room. Have glass bottles filled with an assortment of bath salts, lotions, and perfumes. Place baskets and bowls filled with soaps, bubble baths, and oils by the tub for bathing. Select candles that can be lit if a guest chooses to soak in the tub to relax with a glass of wine or read a favorite novel.

Make certain you have all of the necessities that your guests will need. Extra drinking glasses, plenty of towels, and new bars of soap by the sink should not be forgotten.

Another little secret I have learned is to personally use the guest bathroom before my guests arrive. In that way I know for certain that the drain is draining, that there is plenty of hot water, and that they will have everything they need.

Offering your guests the little extras in the bathroom area will help their stay be easy and worry free. A small night-light in the bathroom makes it easier for the those guests who find it necessary to get up in the middle of the night. Also a small clock that is easy to see makes keeping track of the time convenient.

A large mirror is a necessity but a smaller magnifying mirror is one that will be doubly appreciated by your older guests. Tissue that is easily accessible and extra toothbrushes are items that your guests will find helpful and will appreciate not having to ask for.

Fresh flowers keep an inviting feel in the bathroom. Keep a number of face, hand, and body towels stocked. Be certain there is a place for towels to be hung to dry or deposited after use. If possible, throw bath towels in

the dryer while the guest is showering so they can wrap up in a warm towel when they get out.

Another special touch for the bathroom is a basket full of rose petals, specialty soaps, lemons, and bath salts for the guests to add to their bath as desired.

Be certain to check the bathroom on a daily basis to replenish items that may have been used.

When preparing the bathroom for guests, empty the bathroom drawers and stock them with items your guests may have forgotten or may need during their visit. Each of the items that are placed in the drawers should be new and unused. To save on expenses, buy travel-sized bottles, or keep those that were unused during your last hotel stay.

Top drawer:
Toothbrushes
Toothpaste
Dental floss
Razors
Tweezers
Small scissors
Vaseline
Makeup remover
Assorted makeup:
    eyeshadow, eyeliner,
    concealer, powder,
    lip liner, lipstick
Eye drops
Deodorant
Lotion
Perfume & cologne

Middle drawer:
Baby powder
Bandages & tapes
Calamine lotion
First-aid ointments
Medication:
    antacid, aspirin,
    cold tablets, sleep
    aids, throat
    lozenges, vitamins,
    lip balm
Sunscreen
Votive & scented
    candles
Matches
Bug repellent spray
Cotton balls & swabs

Third drawer:
Back scrub brush
Hairbrush
Cuticle scissors
Emery boards & files
Fingernail polish &
    remover
Nail clippers
Foot creams & scrubs
Hair dryer
Hand mirror
Shoe horn
Shoe-shine supplies:
    brush, cloth, polish,
    cleaner, conditioner,
    water repellent
    spray

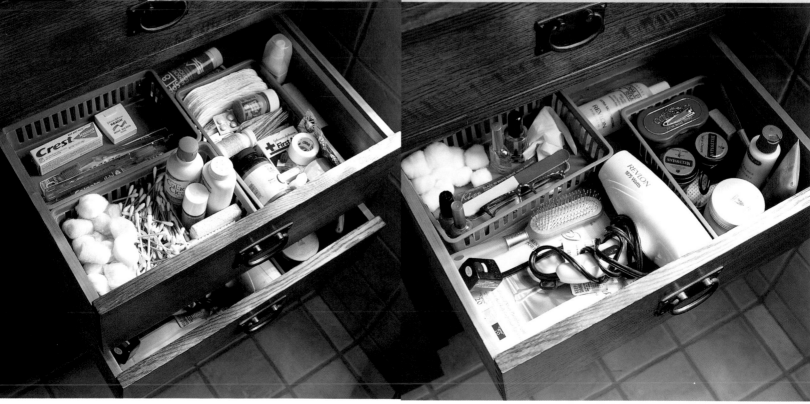

A cupboard in the guest bathroom should also be cleaned out and filled with items with which your guests can pamper themselves. The shelves can be filled with extra towels, a clock and a favorite picture of your guest. It is also here you can display bottles of bath oils, lotions, body sprays, and perfumes. In addition to all of these sometimes necessary items, you could offer your guests items that are meant only to pamper. Foot care and massage products with small written instructions on how to use them and a note inviting them to indulge is a very special touch indeed. It is sometimes that only on vacation do most of us find the time to indulge in such a guilty pleasure.

In some bathroom areas there is room to use small furniture pieces as part of the accent décor. Here a small drawer unit holds the extra boxes and rolls of tissue. A small box on top holds feminine products, while the vintage purse holds candles and matches.

Under the bathroom sink where items are easily located, you will want to supply your guests with a small waste can, additional rolls and boxes of toilet tissue and feminine products. Additionally, keep air freshener, cleaning agents (cleansers, window cleaner, shining agents), disinfectants, sponges, cleaning towels, and scrub brushes. Guests oftentimes will feel more comfortable if they clean their bath area before they leave, but do not feel at ease asking for the supplies.

Not many of us have time on a daily basis to soak in a hot tub and enjoy soft music with a glass of wine or a good book. So this is a perfect gift to give your guests—especially your female family and friends. Have a tray over the tub filled with pampering necessities. Scented quality soaps, bath products meant for soaking and relaxing, special brushes and cloths, candles, a small bowl holding a gardenia, and, of course, on the edge of the tub, leave fresh slippers and luxurious towels to wrap up in when she is finished.

It is also nice, whenever possible, to have a window that will open in the bath area. Many of us like to feel the fresh air and hear the sounds of the morning as the new day begins.

Master Bath & Bedroom

*I*n today's fast-moving world with too many demands, we often neglect to find the time to pamper ourselves and our mate. On a day that is special for no other reason than it just feels right, take the time to do something extra. It is important to do such little niceties on special occasions like anniversaries and birthdays; however, it is more important to remember to do them on any Sunday just to say "I love you." I can promise you that it will mean so much more on an ordinary day than it does on an expected special day.

On an evening that is special for no other reason than you would like to spend time together make some preparations. Be certain you are going to be alone, then draw a scented bath with rose petals floating in the water. Arrange special towels, candlelight, fresh flowers, iced martinis or glasses of wine, decadent desserts, and soft music. Take an hour or two just to enjoy each other and get to know each other again.

If you look closely at the photograph above, you will see that the two halves of this bed are definitely different to accommodate the likes of both parties, yet they look beautiful together. This concept, when carefully planned out, works beautifully from both a comfort and a designer point of view.

Personalize Nightstands

The master bedroom is such a personal space, yet it is also a space that must almost always be shared with one of the most important people in your life. When sharing your bedroom, you must find a way to make it a comfortable, relaxing place for both of you—which is not always an easy goal to accomplish. Some of us like areas that are dark and rich and more masculine in nature; some of us like those decorative items that are beaded or lacy or more feminine. This couple found a way to make it work for both of them. They both enjoy dark rich colors that work well together, so they designed the bed accessories on each side of the bed to be different—yet the same.

The husband's side has a mixture of rich satin and heavily embroidered pillows. His night table has "his" items. A picture of his choosing, a kaleidoscope that is one of his collectibles, an alarm clock he prefers that jolts him awake in the morning, and a selection of books and magazines he enjoys reading.

On the other side of the bed, the wife has chosen those items that fulfill her needs and tastes as well.

75

Loving Him

One idea that will make your spouse feel special is to celebrate your loving him on a day that is not your anniversary or any other special day. Place a fresh bouquet of flowers by the bed, place a souvenir from your wedding day next to his pillow, have a bucket filled with iced glasses and champagne nearby. Buy yourself a beautiful nightie to wear, and scent the bed with roses.

In the morning make heart-shaped waffles and serve them to him in bed. He will love you more for this than you will ever imagine—because it is just for him, just because you love him, and you care enough to take the time to show him.

It is difficult to decorate a bedroom to fit all of the needs and purposes it was designed for. It must be functional for those who use it; a place to relax and heal after a long day in a much too busy world; a place to share with smaller children in the family and help them through nights that frighten them; but also a place for intimate spontaneous togetherness. To attend to all of these needs is no easy task. So creative measures must be used here more than in any other room of the home.

If there is always a plate filled with fresh cookies and a decanter of iced water with glasses by the bed, they can be enjoyed by any number of "guests."

Scented oils, lotions, and candles are nice to have within easy reach for use during anytime of the day or evening.

More personal items can be easily, yet discretely, stored within reach. Some such personal items, where it is important to the owner that no one else use them, are special oils and a massager for sore muscles and health problems. These can be stored in a decorative box that is either displayed openly or slides conveniently under the dresser or the bed. This also works well for more personal romantic items.

79

Simple Touches

Remember to add the special touches that make a difference everyday. Place fresh sheets on the bed—those dried on the clothesline outside have a feel and smell that cannot be bottled. Have slippers placed strategically by the bed and fresh water lightly flavored with slices of oranges, lemons, or limes on the table. It is easy to understand why these extraordinary touches may seem too time consuming or unimportant; but remember, it is the little things that matter and it is the little things that make the biggest difference.

A little extra time in the morning to make coffee, bring in the morning paper, fresh-squeeze juice, and prepare hot croissants will begin a day that has no choice but to be a good day.

Present your spouse with chocolates for breakfast, letting him or her know they are sweet at all hours of the day.

A special touch that will always be appreciated is to put a sachet of a favorite scent in each of the drawers in the bedroom. It is a thoughtful gesture that will gently remind someone throughout the day, as they smell the soft scent of lavender or sandlewood, of someone who cares enough to do something extra.

His & Her Bathroom

A bathroom that is shared by two people should be equipped to fill the needs of both. This bathroom is divided into two halves—one for each—with the products that each enjoys using. There are also coordinating but different cloths, scrubbers, and towels so each knows which is whom's.

Paying attention to these small details, and making certain that your spouse has all of the items that they enjoy using, will make their day begin a little nicer with a little less hassle. This is what all of us can use on any given day.

RIGHT: Not many people can afford the expensive little extras for the house, but this couple splurged and put a television behind the husband's bathroom mirror. The mirror backing was removed just in front of the television screen. Now each morning as he shaves, he can watch his favorite news program.

Arrange the master bathroom for comfort and leisure. Watching your favorite program in a hot bubble bath filled with your favorite bath salts helps take the edge off the day.

Have scented candles positioned in various places around the bathroom. It is a treat to walk into a room that smells of your favorite scent, whether it be gardenias or a more masculine musk.

Daughter's Bedroom

*E*very girl needs a space to call her own. A place where she can decorate the way she chooses, in the colors and styles she likes. It is this place that she can put those treasures and mementos that mean the most to her. Your daughter, or a young woman that has come to live in your home, either temporarily or permanently, needs her own space as much as you do. It will reinforce in quiet ways your love, your trust, and your appreciation of her.

In this instance, you will need to learn to be as diplomatic as possible. There are certain aspects and inclusions that will help in ways your daughter may not understand. For example: there is no better place to curl up with a good book or magazine than in her own private space, tucked away from the hectic everyday goings-on with the house. The ideal spot would be a window seat with good natural light that would also include pillows, a blanket, a small lamp, and a warm cup of hot cocoa. You will

want to make certain that materials are natural and durable to withstand the use and abuse given by either the very young or a teenager.

Do not forget to include a small bouquet of fresh flowers, regardless of the time of year. During the summer months, have your daughter help select her favorite roses or flowering plants, have her help plant them in the garden, and then cut those fresh flowers to add to her room. It is a special touch that teaches as much about gardening as it does about loving and caring. During the winter months, a small bouquet is an inexpensive alternative, either from the grocery store or your local florist.

Decorating with Your Daughter

The look of your daughter's room will change as she gets older. However, regardless of her age, it is important that she chooses how her room will look. You may not always agree, in fact, it is almost a guarantee that it will be difficult for you to do what is requested.

I remember when I was in junior high school, I asked my mother if I could paint and decorate my room the way I wanted. She reluctantly agreed but she let me choose the colors and the furnishings. I painted the walls a very bright chartreuse green and carefully selected cotton candy pink bedspreads, drapes, and rug. My mother had to close the door during the day so she could walk down the hall; but I loved that room—I still love that room. It said and did for me everything a private and personal space should.

Journal Sharing

A friend told me about a special touch that I wish I had done for my daughter as she was growing up. My friend and her daughter went on a small shopping trip together and picked out matching journals—one for each of them. Both would leave their journal and a pen in an easy-to-find place in their bedrooms. When the need or the occasion would arise, each would write the other a small note either to start their day or to end it. It was sometimes a note to wish good luck on an exam or a job interview, sometimes it was to remind them of something important, and sometimes it was to say "thank you" or "I love you" for no reason at all.

I envy my friend and her journal with notes through the years from her daughter. How her life changed; how her handwriting became more controlled and sophisticated; how she shared her ups and downs, and innermost thoughts with her mom—what a treasure day by day and forever.

Little Treasures

Most little girls, big girls, and even older, much wiser "girls" love fancy, feminine, personal things. Such pieces might include accent items that are monogrammed. So why not monogram a pillow for your daughter's room? Take her shopping, listen carefully when she shows you the pillows that she loves, then surprise her with one you have made yourself. It is easy to do, there are hundreds of monogram patterns available, and it is small and portable so that it can be done in the evening hours in front of the television, at your desk during lunch, or on a plane.

Another easy, quick, and thoughtful gift is a handmade card that says "I love you." If you do not know how, you can buy any of the unlimited number of books on the subject. Make it to fit her personality, and give it to her on a small tray with fancy dishes filled with cookies and tea. It is a perfect way to wish her good luck while she is studying for exams, or to help her feel even prettier while she is dressing for the prom.

It is a fast-paced and sometimes dangerous world that our loved ones enter each day; and you cannot always be there to help them or keep them safe. To remind your daughter on a daily basis how much you care, buy tiny silver coins to put in her purse that have angels embossed on them. Every time she opens her purse she will see them and know how much you really do care.

The one wish we all have for our children is that they be watched over so they are kept safe from harm and are given a little extra help in making wise decisions. Place an angel in her room—you may not believe as some do in such things, but it couldn't hurt. And by the angel's side, place a pretty box where you can put notes or cards you have written to her. Or you can buy tiny treasures, wrap them, and leave them in the box every once in a while for her to find.

When was the last time you served your teenage daughter breakfast in bed? I'm not certain if I ever did; and it probably would have had to have been lunch because she loved to sleep in when she wasn't working or in school. Why not one morning, while she is in the shower, place a small tray on her bed with fresh juice, fruit, and a hot croissant. It really doesn't take that much longer, and both of you will be amazed at how much such a small deed can say or do for each of you. And don't forget the fresh flowers.

Everyone loves to be pampered: young and old, male and female, athlete or concert pianist. There is no nicer way to pamper a young lady than with fresh, fancy linens and small bouquets of sweet-smelling flowers. Try placing a tiny bunch of flowers wrapped in satin ribbons on her pillow; it will make her feel remembered and special.

Hot Gingered Appleade

2 quarts apple juice or cider
3 cups water
1 12-oz. can frozen lemonade concentrate
¼ cup sugar
1 tsp. ginger, ground

In a 4-quart saucepot, mix apple juice or cider, water, lemonade concentrate, sugar, and ginger. Over medium-high heat, bring to a boil. Reduce heat to low and simmer for 15 minutes.

Whether studying for tests or returning from a long work day, surprise your daughter with a hot drink and an encouraging card.

A bottle of lavender water is a nice addition for bed linens. All you need do is pour the scented water in a spray bottle so she can mist her sheets and pillowcase before she goes to bed. If your daughter is very small and you read to her at night, do this for her just before the story begins.

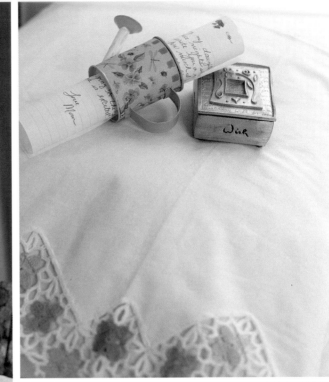

Leave an unexpected snack on her dressing table as a special touch any day. A handwritten note placed on the pillow with a tiny gift box is a nice touch for a mother to do for her daughter. Fill the tiny box with small treasures—an inexpensive pair of earrings, a $5.00 bill for extra spending money, or a good luck charm. Place a lavender sachet in her drawer bringing a gentle lavender scent to her sweaters.

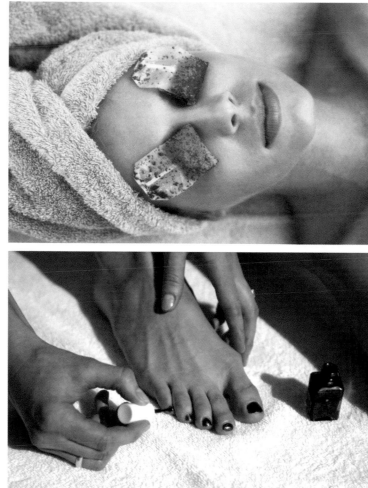

Everyone who exists in today's world lives a life that is filled with an unyielding amount of stress. It matters not the age, or the occupation, or the social status—we all face our own problems and try to overcome our own obstacles. Teenage daughters may have more stress in their lives than adults can even imagine. As mothers, we sometimes pamper ourselves with fancy spas that offer thermal wraps and back massages; but have you ever taken your daughter? If you cannot afford such a luxury, create your own at home. If you buy the necessary supplies, she can either pamper herself alone in the quiet of her room, the two of you can pamper each other, or she can share such fun with her friends. Such a surprise is especially welcome on the weekend of finals, the day before she marries, or on any Sunday afternoon just because she's earned it.

A daughter's bathroom is not always a thing of organization, cleanliness, and beauty. But maybe, just maybe, if the items she had to use were of her choosing, were lovely to look at, and even nicer to pamper herself with . . . then maybe, just maybe, she would keep her bathroom clean.

Buy her soft luxurious towels, designer bath sprays and gels, and fancy perfumes. It used to be that such items could not be afforded, either for ourselves or as gifts—let alone teenage daughters! However, with the popularity of discount stores that sell designer everything for less, these special items do not cost any more than what the no-name brands with unattractive packaging used to cost. And besides, who is more important to you than your own daughter?

93

Son's Bedroom

When you think of extraordinary touches for an ordinary day, the first people to come to mind are: your spouse, a guest, your friends, your daughter, but most often not your son. It isn't because you don't love him or want to pamper him as much as all of these others, it is because your son is the most difficult to know exactly how he would like to be pampered. You would do almost anything he requested; but usually when asked, the reply is "nothing thanks, I'm ok." He simply wants to be left alone or be with his friends. So what do you do for this very special man in your life? Find some small, special touches he may enjoy.

Every bedroom should have a comfortable chair for resting and reading. And it should be placed by a window so there is natural light and fresh air. In addition to the window, make certain there is an adequate lamp and maybe even house slippers. Does your son wear house slippers? Is it because he doesn't have any or can't find them if he does? In the winter, why not place a pair of warm slippers by his chair? You might be surprised.

Surprise your son with a very special snack of café au lait and European cookies. It will be unexpected, yet enjoyed as much as if you were indulging yourself.

94

As in your daughter's room, make certain your son has items that will make his life at home more comfortable, productive, and enjoyable. Provide a desk, with a good light and adequate materials, at which he can study. He needs to be reminded that it is here where he will concentrate best and produce better work. It will prepare him for working in an office someday (if that is what he chooses to do).

Another nice touch is to leave him a note—not telling him what not to forget, but to say something nice and unexpected. Place a bulletin board in his room or by his door in the hall so he can see notes on a daily basis.

While he is studying, pamper him with soup and sandwiches or cookies and hot cocoa. Boys are always hungry, so keep him from going to the kitchen every twenty minutes and pamper him just a little. It is a little thing, but one that he will appreciate.

95

LEFT: Most sons do not often stay in five-star hotels where they turn down your bed and put mints on your pillow—so why not surprise him and do just that. In addition, make a small card from two pieces of cardboard tied with a ribbon. Inside put a note that says how much you love him just for being him and finish with, "sweet dreams and sleep tight," the same way you did when he was two years old.

After your son has decorated his room the way he wants, add a few "little" things to make it even better. Use soft cotton sheets in the summer and warm flannel sheets during the months of winter. Have comfortable pillows, a feather mattress, and don't say anything, ever, about all the dog hair on the bed.

In his room, give him that which keeps him entertained. Your life will be much easier and much quieter if he has his own television, vcr with a supply of acceptable movies, and a CD player with his favorite CDs.

If the room is large enough, supply chairs for his friends to sit in; if not, make certain the covering on his bed is a medium color and durable. There will be lots of lying around by lots of guys who eat lots of greasy food.

Add his own telephone with his own private line. This may sound extravagant, but it was truly the nicest thing I did for myself when my teenagers were at home.

Frame the pictures that mean the most to him. Framing is a nice compromise between the art you would like to see on his walls and the posters he would like to tape to his walls!

Son's Bathroom

A son's bathroom can be a frightening image. I know when I was in college, I used the bathroom at the gas station on the corner rather than using the one in the house where my boyfriend lived (and I know his mother did not raise him that way)!

Do what you can to help him keep it clean without doing it for him. Except maybe once in a while as a special touch in and of itself, just so he won't forget how nice it really can be.

Have a glass with extra toothbrushes by his sink. I don't know what happens to them, but they always seem to disappear. In the shower, be certain there is a good shower head, plenty of hot water, and a place to keep his bathing essentials and toiletries. Remember a mirror for shaving, shaving cream, bottles of shampoo and conditioner, along with bath gels, loofah sponges, and fingernail brushes for scrubbing.

A small gift you can give your son is a water-proof radio to listen to while showering. Usually with the water running he can turn it up as loud as he would like and not bother anyone.

When decorating his bathroom make it rustic and as maintenance-free as possible. You do not want any fragile glass fixtures that will break or white towels to use. Keep a candle with a supply of matches, but check it daily because he may forget to blow it out.

Just as with the bedroom, let your son's personality and interests shine through in the decor of his bathroom. His opinion matters and his tastes are unique, let him enjoy his individuality. This will help him feel good about himself and his tastes as well as give him an incentive to keep the room in better shape to show off his treasures.

Laundry Room

*T*he laundry room is the one room in the house that should be used by everyone—often. It should be large enough to adequately do its job. It should be decorated in a way that makes it a comfortable place to be, and it should have many of the niceties as in the other rooms of the house.

Do not decorate your laundry room last or with the least imagination. You should love to be in this room to do the chores, to "fuss around," and not be embarrassed if your guests need to wash a few things or borrow the iron.

Have a clock on the wall, put detergent in a fancy container like the shell vase shown to the left, paint the walls a bright faux finish, and consider hanging a picture or two on the wall.

Laundry rooms are often in the basement and therefore very dark. So do whatever is necessary to not only lighten and brighten, but warm it up. It is a nice thing to do not only for others but for yourself.

Have a place to hang the clothes that either should not go in the dryer or that have been just ironed. Have all of the supplies you need in a safe place (out of the reach of small children), distinctively marked, and in "designer" jars.

If the laundry room is stocked with the right equipment and materials, doing the laundry can actually be a job you look forward to.

A special touch for those doing laundry is the addition of a small television with a vcr and a supply of movies.

Laundry room supplies:

Stain remover

Small scrub brush

Bleach

Detergents for delicate & normal
    clothing

Softener

Iron & ironing board

Spray starch

Spray bottle with water

Scented water for spraying on linens
    & sheets

Hangers of several types (skirt, pant,
    blouse)

Clothesline or hanging rack

Baskets for carrying clothes

Rags

Individual clothes hampers

Scented candles or potpourri

Fresh flowers

It seems that putting the clothes away after they are laundered is a task that everyone avoids. Why not put a note saying thank you and a treat for whoever takes the basket upstairs and puts everything away.

Supply nice hampers that breathe for dirty clothes. Label each hamper so everyone knows not to put the wet towels or dirty jeans in with your expensive silk blouse.

Outside

Every garden, regardless of its size, should have small walking paths, a variety of plants, and an array of interesting garden art. One of the nicest pieces of garden art is an angel—to protect all who live in or enter the garden. Put her in a quiet place by a chair or bench so that visitors or family members can sit in this very special place for just a while.

For those of us who spend most of our time indoors—whether working, traveling, or attending school—it is a special treat to spend time out-of-doors. Which is only one of the reasons why it is so important to make the outside of your home as welcoming, comfortable, and useful as the inside. Whether you design and decorate this area to fulfill your own needs, to pamper your guests, or to give your children another place to enjoy, you should add those special touches that make it a special place for everyone.

A small table on the patio with a lovely but durable tablecloth is a quiet and welcome retreat for anyone. It can be a place to eat a late lunch, read the last chapter of a good book, or just enjoy the sunset.

On a nearby chair, float scented candles and tiny blossoms in a bowl. Do not forget why porch swings used to be so popular. They are a wonderful special touch for family and friends to enjoy. Add a holder filled with current newspapers and magazines, a tray with cool drinks and snacks, and a book or two and this is a place that will be used and enjoyed often.

Outdoor Fun

When family and guests are enjoying the outdoors, it is simple to add little extras. Place a jug of iced water and a basket of fresh fruit outside the window to give anyone in the yard a quick snack. Simple flavored ice pops placed in a bowl of ice are affordable and appreciated. And any outdoor activity should be celebrated with homemade ice cream and fresh fruit. This is always a special treat—regardless of the time or the reason.

Have you ever laid in a hammock on a quiet afternoon and listened to the birds sing while you napped or read your favorite book? If you have, you know why this is the epitome of an "extraordinary touch for an ordinary day." If you haven't, then purchase a hammock and treat yourself to one of the most wonderful small touches of all.

When adult guests bring their children or when young friends come over to play, it is thoughtful and much appreciated to have something for little visitors to do. What you buy to entertain them need not be elaborate or expensive. Children oftentimes have the most fun with something that allows them to use their imagination. Small, easily purchased, and conveniently stored items such as those featured in the surrounding photographs, will turn your home into a favorite place to visit.

Pets

Every pet should have a place of its own to sleep and maybe a friend to share the day with. Pets, just like humans, can become lonely when left home alone all day.

Have a special place for your family pet to feel comfortable in front of a warm window where it can see out.

F or some, their pets are the only family they have; for others, they are second only in importance to the rest of the family members. Still others have pets for a variety of their own personal reasons. However, for almost all owners, their pets are definitely an important part of their daily lives and they deserve a little extraordinary touch for an ordinary day as much as anyone else.

Take the time to indulge your pets once in a while. After all, they love you unconditionally with devotion that is worthy of a special reward.

Remember that animals were not meant to be cooped up all day, alone in the house while their owners are at work or "out" having their own good time. Take your dog to work with you for the day—he will love the change of scenery and the new faces. Teach your dog a new trick or two. Painting may be a little further than you would like to go, but you would be amazed at what dogs can learn how to do. Always take them for a walk, and sometimes maybe even a ride. It is what nature intended, even for domestic animals—so do not forget what they not only "want" but honestly require to be healthy and happy.

Animals are very important to their owners and, like the other "people" in their owners' lives, they want to remember their pets. Sometimes for very special reasons and sometimes for no reason at all.

Take your pet's picture, either professionally or with your own camera, have it framed, and hang it in an appropriate room. It is less expensive than an original piece of art and it means so much more.

When doing something extraordinary for the feline in your life, why not go over the top—just once in a while. Put her food and water into crystal dishes, and place these on a silver serving tray with candles and a bouquet of fresh roses.

Sometimes, doing something a little bit special for the animals in your life is doing something special for yourself as well. There is little that is more cumbersome and unsightly than bags of dog food. They are heavy, they spill easily, and they smell like dog food. Why not put each type of dog food in a small silver trash can right next to the dog bowls—which, of course, are also silver. In this way, the food is easy to get to, the smell is concealed, and the room looks wonderful.

Add a pillow or two for your dog to sleep on. Few of us can afford expensive dog beds, yet two tapestry floor pillows can be purchased inexpensively at a discount store. The tapestry is easy to wipe off and it shows little or no dog hair. Or take two or three old pillows with soft worn pillowcases and "make" your dog a bed of his own.

111

Grandma's House

*M*ake coming to grandma's house an anticipated event. Provide opportunities for grandchildren to learn new things, let them drive a tractor, ride a horse, or take a taxi. Allow them to experience whatever environment you live in. This will not only broaden children's knowledge, but create a memorable time together that your grandchildren will remember for years to come.

Grandma—with a constant smile, a supply of our favorite baked goodies, and plenty of surprises— knows how to make an ordinary day extraordinary.

As a grandma, have a special place in your kitchen reserved just for grandchildren. This anticipated area will become the first place they run to when visiting, to find something special waiting for them. It doesn't have to be their birthday, or be a "big" gift, it is just some little thing that grandma saw that she knew each one would like. Keep each small treasure or treat in a sack with the child's name on it in a special holder. These little gifts of thoughtfulness are truly extraordinary gifts for an ordinary day.

Keep each grandchild's favorite candy on hand especially for them, or know and stock each grandchild's favorite ice cream in the freezer with their own name on the box. Certainly you may have a few different boxes of ice cream in the freezer; however, this is a wonderful way to let each child know they are important and individual, and you respect that and love them for it.

Rather than serving malts from the blender, have old-fashioned sodas. Show children how they use to enjoy this treat at the malt shops. Let them experiment with different flavorings. Remember the straws and old-fashioned glasses.

Movie Time

Make events special for the grandchildren by adding to the event. When watching a movie together, have a large selection of videos that are entertaining and still acceptable to the parents. You don't have to overrule parents' rules to still have a great time. Coordinate movies with projects and snacks. For example, serve malts in old-fashioned malt glasses with licorice-stick straws. Place these on old LP records for all to enjoy while watching the movie Grease or another period movie the children may enjoy.

Another way to enjoy the show would be by making a project together during the movie. Create a "money box" or "money frame" to store or frame pictures taken of the evening's fun while watching a show such as Risky Business.

Money Box

1. Tape dollar bills together, forming a 10" x 12" rectangle for shirt. Center shirt on top of shirt box lid and secure in place.

2. To form collar, tape two dollar bills together. Fold bills in half lengthwise and secure together in front.

3. To make a tie, fold the corners at one end of a dollar bill into a point. Fold dollar bill sides under to finish length if tie. Secure tie to shirt top.

4. To form pocket, fold one dollar bill in half widthwise and secure to shirt.

5. Fold one dollar bill in half lengthwise then in half widthwise. Tuck inside pocket on shirt.

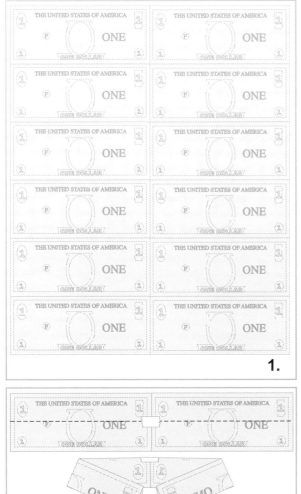

1.

2. **3.** **4.** **5.**

Memorable Moments

Small extraordinary touches can be the memorable moments that are created for those we love on no special day at all.

It isn't necessary to have a birthday cake only on a birthday. Why not have a "party" just to celebrate an ordinary day. For the younger ones, it is a memorable event if they are given a cake of their own to eat without inhibition or restriction . . . and don't forget the party hats!

celebrating a Half Birthday

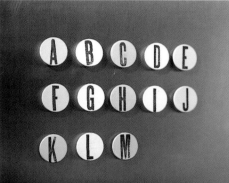

Birthdays are special and anticipated times, especially by young children. An extraordinary touch to remind children that they are special all year long is to surprise them with a half-birthday party. On the day exactly six months from their true birth date, surprise them with a party including half of a birthday cake and gifts that are separated in half. You may choose to give the child the first half of alphabet magnets or a bookmark, giving them the remaining magnets and a book the following day.

For the little girls who love to dress up, one glove, one earring, one shoe, and half of a game of jacks makes a great gift. This silliness can be enjoyed all day.

This type of surprise is certainly not exclusive to children. Have fun surprising your spouse or a friend with a half-day celebration inviting her friends to a "half luncheon." Challenge the guests to think up their own half-gift ideas for the guest of honor and enjoy the imagination of the gifts that are shared.

117

Dressing Up

When I was very young, I wore my mother's jewelry and it made me feel beautiful. When my daughter was young she made me a plaque in school that read: "Mother, wears pretty clothes, makes needlecraft books, and makes me feel special." When we are young, we want to dress up, look older, and be as pretty as our mothers—which I think is why little girls love to play dress-up. There is nothing more fun than to have a box of clothes in a grown-ups closet that can be explored on rainy afternoons. The boxes can be marked with tags on beaded chains and placed within a child's reach. In that way, whether they be your own children, grandchildren, or the children of friends, they will know there is someplace special that holds something special just for them.

118

Growing Up

Only when you are young do you want to grow up; and even though as adults we wish it didn't happen so quickly, it is important for us to "mark" the days and the inches that our children grow. To make it special, mark it in a place that is important to the child, where he can see it on a daily basis, because he wants to check every single day to see how big he is.

To make it even more of an event, hang a diary on the wall next to the yardstick and write down what happened on the day the child grew one more inch. It is such a little extra touch that makes a child feel important and "all grown up."

Offering a Helping Hand

In our busy worlds with too little time and too much to do, fast food, prepackaged dinners, and dining out have become a way of life. Seldom do we take the time to make homemade pies from scratch or chocolate chip cookies the old-fashioned way. Spending time in the kitchen making such delightful desserts can be such a special time.

I can remember my mother telling me stories of her and my grandmother spending cold winter afternoons in the kitchen baking pies for dinner. They weren't special dinners like Thanksgiving or Christmas, they were simply weekday meals and the preparation, at the time, seemed more like a chore than an event. But looking back, they were some of the nicest times my mother remembers spending with her mother. Maybe it is time to take an afternoon off and spend it in the kitchen baking something "special" for dinner with the younger members of your family. They will learn something new, share something special, and serve something wonderful. It is a little thing that can create many happy memories.

Playing

Whether in the kitchen or out in the field, an afternoon spent between a child and a parent can be the most memorable and rewarding of all. Every child wants to be better at sports, to have fun at what they play, and to share their victories or their defeats with those they love the most. Take time, a couple of afternoons or evenings a week, to throw a ball, catch a butterfly, or snag a fish. Think about it, an hour three times a week really isn't that much time to invest in someone and something that is so important.

Marshmallow Popcorn

½ cup corn syrup
2 sticks margarine
2 cups sugar
4 cups popped corn
½ bag miniature marshmallows

In a saucepan, bring corn syrup, sugar, and margarine to a boil over low heat. Let boil for 5 minutes until sugar dissolves. Mix marshmallows into popcorn. Pour syrup mixture over popcorn and marshmallows and stir to coat.

Having a Slumber Party

Sleep-overs are as much a part of being young and growing up as going to school and falling in love. From make-up make-overs to painting fingernails, to braiding each other's hair, there is nothing quite like an all-girl all-nighter. And it is so easy to make each one special. Homemade marshmallow popcorn, special pillowcases to take home, pancakes made to look like your best friend.

Give a disposable camera to the "hostess" and have her take pictures of the night's activities. Keep each sleep-over in an album—these will be some of the fondest memories a daughter will have with her friends in the years to follow.

Be prepared for the evening, stocking up with curlers, bath beads, lip balm, fingernail polish, and travel bottles of shampoo. For younger girls, supply colored pencils, pens, stickers, and scrapbooks.

Make a CD of their favorite music for them to dance to, or plan a treasure hunt. Prepare supplies for the girls to make something together, such as fabric paint to autograph oversized T-shirts to wear as pajamas, or make cupcakes to eat during a favorite movie.

Creating a Family Formal Dinner

Remember when you were small and you watched, from afar, grown-ups having fancy dinner parties and you wished you were involved. You imagined how pretty you would look or how important you would feel. Why not have a fancy dinner party for members of your family on a day that you are celebrating nothing at all. Have the children dress up in their finest attire and set the table as if the Queen herself were coming. It is so important to take the time to do for those closest to us what we do for others.

Pick an evening when the entire family can come. Create a formal invitation and leave it in each family member's room where they will be certain to see it the day before the party.

Add to the special evening with the family by dressing up in fine clothes. The smaller members of the family may not want to dress up in their own clothes but those they "dream" of wearing to fancy dinner parties! Find suitable grown-up clothes for them to wear to this grown-up meal.

During the meal, make a toast to the members of your family—when you are finished you might have someone at the table make a toast of their own. Plan ahead so that something special can be said. This will be the per-

fect time for the younger members of the family to learn proper "toasting" etiquette—how to participate in one and how to make one. And don't forget to serve exotic foods and use the finest linens, silver, and crystal. A fancy dinner such as this must have every detail attended to.

Place cards are a formality that are a must at such an elegant affair. There is a number of ways to make a place card that is simple, inexpensive, and memorable.

A tiny silver frame can hold each person's name. During the evening, pictures can be taken, then placed inside the frame later.

Plain votive candleholders can have each person's name written in calligraphy on the outside. After being formally seated, the candles can be placed at the head of each plate and the lights can be dimmed.

For a special touch, serve the meal in courses. This would be a perfect time to teach little ones and young adults about table etiquette, table settings, and what each utensil and dish is used for.

You may want to surprise your guests by serving dessert first. A chocolate fondue served with strawberries, bananas, and marshmallows makes for a sweet beginning.

To make the dining event more memorable, do the unusual and the extraordinary. Serve salt in tiny silver bowls with miniature vintage salt spoons, sugar in fancy crystal jars, and butter on the finest of china.

Have a nice selection of wines for the adults and have an equally fine selection of crystal and beverages for the younger children. To resemble their adult counterparts, they could sample apple juice, cranberry juice, nonalcoholic wine, etc. It is important that they have the same number of glasses with similar looking beverages poured at the appropriate times. This is a good time to discuss which wine goes with what food and why—without anyone even knowing they are learning the valuable lessons they will need later in life.

Dinner can consist of family favorites or dishes normally served only on holidays, or you can treat your family to exotic or unusual foods they have not had before. Regardless, the table is set for an extraordinary dining experience.

Sharing Afternoon Tea

There are moments that are so very special they will never be forgotten. Here, on a beautiful afternoon in early summer, a tea party was planned for a great-grandmother of 97 and her great granddaughter. It was not a special day, no one's birthday, no one's graduation, it was simply an everyday afternoon when two "ladies", who on a daily basis share little but who love each other very much, decided to dress up and enjoy a "spot of tea." The table was set with grandma-great's finest laces, linens, and china; tiny sandwiches and crumpets were made; homemade iced peach lemonade was poured into tall crystal glasses; handpainted cookies were served; and two friends spent the afternoon with only each other. No one else knows for certain what was discussed, what was decided, or what was even considered; all that is known is that laughter filled the air and there were knowing smiles and long hugs when the afternoon came to an end.

129

Touching Touches

For yourself

E xtraordinary touches for an ordinary day—do you always do them for someone else, or once in a while do you do something special just for yourself? For a few, a special touch is something indulgent such as a day at the spa. For others, it is something extravagant like a new dress; and for still others, it is that little something extra that you do just for yourself such as jumping in all the puddles.

Do something special for yourself and then do something for someone else.

Just for yourself—
buy a new hat . . .

simply do nothing at all . . .

or discover something new . . .

enjoy watering the plants . . .

smell the flowers . . .

play in the leaves . . .

break the rules . . .

make a wish . . .

relax . . .

133

take a chance . . .

schedule a vacation . . .

soak your feet . . .

134

enjoy learning . . .

love your country . . .

explore the world . . .

For Others

Nothing is more rewarding than doing something
for someone else. Challenge someone to a race . . .

take a friend to the beach . . .

share a secret . . .

be part of a team . . .

clown around . . .

walk daddy home from work . . .

teach someone something new . . .

call a friend . . .

give a hand to someone in need . . .

hug a friend . . .

send your love an
unexpected letter . . .

show someone the way . . .

There are so many extraordinary touches we take for granted in our daily lives. We think about doing them, we often actually think we did them; but how many times in a week do you give someone a helping hand to show them the way or a hug just to say "I love you" for no reason at all? It is the most extraordinary touch of all for any ordinary day.

Conversion Charts

1 ounce	28.35 grams
1 pound	453.59 grams
1 tablespoon	½ fluid ounce
¼ cup	60 ml
½ cup	120 ml
1 cup	240 ml

inches	mm	cm
1	25	2.5
2	51	5.1
3	76	7.6
4	102	10.2
5	127	12.7
6	152	15.2
7	178	17.8
8	203	20.3
9	229	22.9
10	254	25.4
11	279	27.9
12	305	30.5

Acknowledgments

The publishers wish to thank the following for use of their projects, homes, businesses, or photographs:

Marie Browning: p 62—as featured in her book *Beautiful Handmade Soaps*

Corbis Corporation Images © 1999

Chris & Jill Dahlberg

Digital Stock Corporation © 1997

Scott & Julie Dixon

Ralph & Diana Dunkley

Steve & Peggy Fishburn

Richard & Jill Grover

Brad Mee

Chip & Carol Nelson

Jo Packham

Luciana Pampalone: pp 2, 6, 67(ul), 86(ul), 89(br), 102(ul)

Dino Tonn Photography: p 37(ul)

Dr. Harold Vonk

Photodisc, Inc. Images © 1997, 1998, 1999, 2000

Keep a special place to store your favorite items and collectibles. This heart collection can be kept close by the bed and enjoyed by the owner whenever she desires.

Index